Mastering Your
CIRCUS

REFINING CREATIVITY
IN YOUR REAL ESTATE CAREER

LISA JOHNSON JUDEN

Clovercroft Publishing

Published by Clovercroft Publishing, Franklin, Tennessee
www.clovercroftpublishing.com

Edited by Ann Tatlock

Cover design by Jerry Comandante

Interior Design by Suzanne Lawing

Photographer - Jackie Ritz Brickley and Kylie Butler with Focus Creative Photography

ISBN: 978-1-956370-11-9

Printed in the United States of America

*To my mother, Kathleen,
and my husband, Edward,*

I wish to share my deepest gratitude to both of you, my incredible and talented mother, Kathleen, and my amazing and loving husband, Edward. Your unwavering love and support have been the driving force behind the completion of this book. Thank you for believing in me and being by my side during this incredible journey.

Mom, your invaluable editing assistance and guidance have shaped me as an author, and I feel privileged to follow in your footsteps.

Edward, my love, your patience and encouragement have been the cornerstone of my progress. Thank you for pushing me to make this book happen.

Without both of you cheering me on, I could not have written this book, nor achieved this goal or fulfilled my dream. I cherish and adore you both.

Special Thanks

To all my amazing superstars.

Photographer- Kylie Butler with Focused Creative Photography and Jackie Ritz Brickey

Graphic Designer- Jerry Comandante and Blane Richard

Makeup Artist- Lisa Watson

Talent- Aaron Wing, Brittany Couch, Crystal and Dani Cunningham, Daniel Vejman, Dolly Stoddart, Elena Thompson, Greg Anders, Jeff Jannasch, Jerry Johnson, Lori Cecil, Mandy O'Neill, Micah and Cameron Clayton, Nelli Abzaletdinova, Nikki Winders, Reena Patel, Simone Francis, and Stephanie Allen.

Contents

HABITS
ORGANIZED
ETIQUETTE
POP-BY`S
SOCIAL MEDIA
ROUTINES
COMMUNITY
CELEBRATE
DATABASE
CHALLENGES

One

MASTERING YOUR CIRCUS: UNLEASHING YOUR CREATIVE RINGLEADER

In the world of real estate, a real estate agent is like the star performer in a circus. We are the ringleaders who are constantly at the center of the stage, herding clients, training, guiding and showing them love. But let's admit it — being an agent can be overwhelming. We face multiple tasks that demand our attention all at once, making our job a constant juggling act. And let's face it – some of us juggle better than others. Over the years, I've become a pretty adept juggler, so now I want to pass my know-how on to you.

I wrote this book as a guiding light for all my fellow agents, whether you are a seasoned professional or just starting out your journey.

However, the lessons within can benefit anyone embarking on a new career or looking to grow their own business.

Because the life of a real estate agent is a constant whirlwind, much like that of a circus ringleader, my goal is to make your journey smoother.

I've created this book with checklists and challenges, tricks and tips to keep you on track and for you to apply to your business. It's an easy-to-follow guide designed to help you be the best version of yourself and to keep up with everything you need to do.

My aim is to prepare you thoroughly, keep you organized, and ensure you're doing all the right things. I understand that this book may not resonate with everyone, but if you can take away a couple of valuable insights, we're already winners.

Throughout these pages, I will share as much knowledge as I can so that you'll become a creative guru by the time you finish reading.

People will marvel at your cleverness and creativity, wondering where you acquired such skills.

In *Mastering Your Circus,* I have sought to create a resource for real estate agents who need that extra push to reach the next level. I hope to encourage you to engage in some "out of the box" thinking. Get ready to tap into your creative potential and join your own circus — with you as the ringleader!

Not everyone is naturally inclined toward creativity, and that's okay. My goal is to inspire you in your thinking, to be your magic act, and open the doors to my world of creativity.

Throughout the chapters, you'll find challenges to spark your imagination, and you can even scan QR codes for motivational videos.

We all need some encouragement, and I want to be your biggest cheerleader.

Having achieved my real estate dreams, I am now shifting my focus from buying and selling to becoming your mentor and ringleader. My life's passion is to help others succeed.

Allow me to guide you and help you develop fabulous ideas that will set your business apart from competitors. This book is your fast-track ticket to being the very best agent you can be.

Are you ready to take center stage and shine? Let's embark on this creative journey together! Let's go!

Scan to see my personal video.

Two

BIG TOP PEE WEE: THE OPENING ACT

For myself, my circus began when I was 24 years old back in 2000. I was no trick rider, to say the least. However, I did have my own tricks and failures to deal with for sure.

Real estate wasn't my primary consideration for a career when I was 24 years old. In fact, the concept of being an agent wasn't even on my radar. I can't even recall ever personally knowing a real estate agent. Since my family and I resided in the same house for 24 years, I never had the opportunity to experience the process of selling a home firsthand. I had no idea of all that was involved in the process of buying and selling houses.

When I was a young girl, I had a dream of creating my own orphanage, inspired by watching the movie *Annie* countless times on television. My heart went out to all the girls in orphanages, and I imagined becoming a kind and caring Miss Hannigan figure, showering them with love, beautiful clothes, and joyful experiences like singing and dancing.

However, as life unfolded, God had a different path in store for me.

It all started after graduating from the University of North Texas in Denton in 2000, with a degree in art and a minor in marketing. Selling my ceramic bowls alone wasn't enough to make ends meet, and I wanted a more fulfilling job that aligned with my purpose. I reached out to everyone I knew, seeking opportunities every day.

Working as a beverage cart girl at the golf course I was employed at, did have advantages.

Fortunately, the golf course provided me with opportunities to expand my professional connections. Nevertheless, my career took an unexpected turn when a golf ball went through the windshield of my beverage cart and hit me right in the forehead, resulting in 13 stiches.

This incident essentially marked the conclusion of my time in that role. I felt prepared to transition into a new phase of life, one that was more purposeful and not quite as dangerous.

Shortly after the incident, Tim Spurgeon, a regular at the golf course, guided me to an interview at Huntington and Highland Homes in Carrollton's Coyote Ridge, and I was hired as a sales assistant. The houses I showcased were stunning, and it was rewarding to witness potential buyers being captivated by their beauty while also expressing their preferences.

From my office in the model home, I had the chance to listen to the experienced sales counselor, interact with visitors, and share insights about the houses, the neighborhood, the city, and the mortgage process. Those two years were a learning experience, and I realized that real estate was a perfect fit for me. It combined my love for working with people and my love for design, and beautiful homes. An added bonus was the flexibility of managing my own schedule. All of this together gave me a sense of peace.

In pursuit of my real estate license in 2004, I faced several challenges, including being averse to taking tests. The real estate exam was particularly daunting, and despite thinking I was prepared, I failed the national part after successfully passing the state part.

It became a tough journey, as I repeatedly attempted the exam, failing by a mere point each time. The emotional toll was heavy, and I felt embarrassed and disappointed each time I had to inform my friends and family that I hadn't passed yet.

Fortunately, fate intervened when my next-door neighbor, a real estate instructor, discovered my struggles. He generously offered his help, and during a dinner session that lasted four or five hours, he imparted valuable knowledge. Armed with his guidance, I attempted the test again and this time, to my immense relief, I passed! It was a moment of triumph, a testament to perseverance, and the support of a true godsend.

Through this challenging process, I had moments of doubt, questioning whether I would ever succeed. Was real estate for me? Is this a sign? I refused to give up, and the neighbor's timely assistance made all the difference. I will forever be grateful to him and believe he will be one of the five people I meet in Heaven, as described in Mitch Albom's book, *The Five People You Meet in Heaven.*

If you haven't seen the movie adaptation of this book, I highly recommend watching it for its profound messages.

So my opening act in this circus of real estate was a bit rocky, but I forged ahead and eventually I made it. I'm telling you my story to encourage you—whether you're trying to pass the real estate tests, or gain new clients, or make a sale. Don't give up! Perseverance is the key to success in all areas of our lives.

Three

THE STRONGMAN: THE ACT OF CREATING GOOD HABITS AND ROUTINES

Like the strongman, you have to get up and create a routine that works for you. You know the strongman had to spend hours and hours in the gym trying to get stronger and stronger every day.

You have to exercise to form good habits and routines. Not only for your body but your mind as well. You can't go flabby and become lazy; that will get you nowhere.

Do you have an effective routine or system that works well for you? Are you cultivating positive habits for your business and personal life? Establishing a morning routine is crucial.

They say it takes 21 days to form a habit. If you do something consistently for three weeks, you are likely to continue doing it. Give it a try. Settle on a habit that will be beneficial to your life and determine to do it for 21 days and see if it doesn't become a regular part of your routine! "I believe it will!"

Personally, I cherish waking up early and consider it the "Golden Hour." During this time, I feel undisturbed and capable of achieving anything. My morning routine starts with drinking warm lemon water to rehydrate my body after a good night's sleep. I check my phone briefly for any urgent messages, mostly from family, but I try not to linger on it.

Instead, I find a comfortable spot on my back patio and dive into my daily devotional reading, which also includes a time of prayer and gratitude. One of the devotionals I've enjoyed is by Zach Windahl titled *The Bible Study: A One-Year Study of The Bible and How it Relates to You.* I have also read and loved several devotionals by Candace Cameron Bure, Priscilla Shirer, and Lysa TerKeurst, among others. To me, this quiet time is the best part of my day.

Maybe you like to journal? I know a lot of people who love to write things down because it helps them organize their thoughts and feelings on paper. This brings clarity to their dreams, goals, and plan. Purchase a book and start journaling.

Writer Ellie Claire has a great 365-day devotional journal called Just Breathe. I love that one and it takes 5 minutes every day.

Whatever you do, make sure you practice and appreciate everything you have and do!

"GRATITUDE IS THE HEALTHIEST OF ALL HUMAN EMOTIONS. THE MORE YOU EXPRESS GRATITUDE FOR WHAT YOU HAVE, THE MORE LIKELY YOU WILL HAVE EVEN MORE TO EXPRESS GRATITUDE FOR."

—Zig Ziglar

After my time with the Lord, I like to engage in a workout to energize my body. I use YouTube or workout apps that offer fun challenges, like those by Bailey Brown. I love her Pilates workouts! Spending just 15-20 minutes exercising prepares me for the day ahead. By this time, my husband is usually awake, and it's time for breakfast.

My daily routine during the work week begins with activities that I enjoy. It helps me focus better, as opposed to waking up with an alarm or waking up late and rushing around.

Ensuring I go to bed early contributes to feeling refreshed and prepared for the day.

I practice fasting from about 6:30 p.m. (after dinner) until 8 a.m. the next day. Breakfast is a must for me, and is typically a smoothie, juice, or chocolate protein drink, which keeps me going until lunch time.

Around 9 a.m., I make a mushroom coffee with a little bit of creamer, honey, and a dash of cinnamon. This helps my anxiety and really helps me focus. I have noticed a drastic difference drinking Ryze coffee. Ryze is a coffee alternative made with a combination of coffee, medium-chain triglyceride (MCT) oil, and a blend of mushrooms.

Now I'm ready to begin my day. Checking my calendar, I review my schedule to determine whether I'll be working from home, going to early appointments, or heading into the office.

Making a to-do list helps me keep track of tasks and responsibilities. If I have appointments, I make sure I'm ready to leave my house by 9 a.m. When working in the office, I set a schedule and make sure to interact with colleagues to learn from them and get my work done so I can leave the office by 3 p.m.

On most days, I am home by 3:30 p.m. I love to get home, unwind, and start dinner by 6 p.m. The most important break I have is Happy Hour at 5 p.m., with either a glass of wine, rum and Coke, or a poppi (a non-alcoholic drink). This is when I hear about my husband's day, and he usually gets an earful from the day I have had. Seriously, it's always a circus!

It's important to find time to communicate with your spouse, so I cherish that time. We do have one rule, though: "NO PHONES OUT DURING DINNER!"

Throughout my 23 years in this business, I've witnessed people coming and going. It's sad when agents spend so much time, energy and money trying to succeed and then just fail. That is one of the reasons I wrote this book. I want to help them.

Those who don't establish good habits, attend meetings, or stay informed about the market tend to struggle. To be a successful real estate agent requires preparation, dedication, and continuous learning. Many agents became complacent during the COVID period, but it's essential to get back to the basics and return to the office.

Being a successful agent is "easier said than done." It isn't always about showing beautiful homes, dealing with the perfect clients, and having easy closings. Real Estate definitely has its challenges. It's tough to compete, tough to keep up with everything, and it can be a bit crazy.

In fact, 87 percent of real estate agents fail, and there's a reason for this. Knowing the mistakes agents make can help you not to repeat them. Analyzing how others have failed will help you in the long run, and can equip you to prepare and grow a successful business.

Pay attention to the next chapters and take notes.

The show must go on and being prepared is the key.

In our fast-moving business of real estate, maintaining a regular schedule is challenging, as our clients often dictate our time. We find ourselves anxiously checking our phones to avoid missing important messages from clients or waiting until late hours for responses on offers or repairs. The overwhelming influx of emails only adds to the pressure, making it difficult to keep up with everything. Do you ever feel like you can't keep up?

However, it's essential not to let these demands consume us. Learning to set boundaries is crucial — realizing that our time matters just as much as our clients'. It took me awhile to learn to say "no" to my clients, and remind myself that they are on my schedule. It is hard but you set the stage.

Effective communication is paramount in each transaction. I make it a point to keep my clients informed if I am going to be unavailable for an entire day or traveling out of town.

However, avoiding the whirlwind of chaos requires thorough preparation. Even when we're slammed with work, we have to take care that all the tools of our trade are organized and updated; that is, ensuring that all buyer and seller packets are ready, updating marketing materials during slower periods, staying informed about current rates and market trends, planning showings in advance, and having a clean car and marketing materials ready are vital!

Being a prepared real estate agent is non-negotiable.

Get organized – Create a dedicated workspace for yourself and gather all your equipment to make sure it is organized and in one place. To facilitate the process, I've created a dedicated bag that contains everything I need for listing and showing homes. It is actually a diaper bag I bought on Amazon with a lot of side pockets and dividers. It's the best!

It includes: thank-you note cards, blue tape for new construction homes, a clipboard for clients to jot down notes during showings, a tape measure, flashlight, notepad, pens, breath mints, booties, masks, hand sanitizer, highlighters, gifts for sellers, personal brochures, brand books, handwipes, screws for riders, clear sheet protectors for listing books, and even rain boots and a raincoat for unpredictable weather. This way, with my bag at hand, I am not losing my mind trying to find it all at the last minute.

I am not saying go out and get a diaper bag, but make sure that everything you need is all in one place.

In the end, the key to thriving in this fast-paced business is to be well-prepared and organized. By setting boundaries and keeping communication channels open, we can ensure that "the show will go on" smoothly, providing the best service to our clients at all times.

In conclusion, being proactive and establishing positive habits have been factors in my success as an agent. I hope the knowledge and experiences I've gained over the years can help you in your own journey.

Your show must go on! Again, being prepared is the ultimate key to thriving in this business. If you learn anything from this book, make sure you are prepared at all times.

Don't get lazy, stay strong and create a routine that works for you. And remember the strongman didn't get strong overnight!

What are some better habits and routines you need to start incorporating daily to be more prepared and organized?

_____

_____

_____

_____

_____

_____

_____

_____

_____

_____

_____

_____

Listing

CHECKLIST

- ☐ BOOTIES FOR SHOWINGS IN A BASKET
- ☐ BREATHMINTS
- ☐ CLEAR SHEETS FOR YOUR LISTINGS BOOK FOR SDN AND SURVEY
- ☐ CLIPBOARD
- ☐ FLASHLIGHT
- ☐ GIFT FOR SELLERS/ THANK YOU NOTE
- ☐ HANDSANITIZER/MASK/ WIPES
- ☐ LOCKBOX/ SIGN/ FLYER BOX (IF YOU USE THEM)
- ☐ MEASURING DEVICE FOR ROOM MEASUREMENTS
- ☐ NOTEBOOK
- ☐ NOTEPAD AND PEN
- ☐ RAIN BOOTS - FOR RURAL AREAS
- ☐ RUBBER MALLET FOR SIGN
- ☐ SCREWS FOR THE RIDER
- ☐ WELCOME SIGN

Four

THE HUMAN CANNONBALL: CRAFTING A NEW "YOU"

Are you a Human Cannonball? Do you still shoot out old marketing material over and over again? Is everything outdated?

Well, if so, it is time to quit thinking you have that safety net to catch you. It is time to create a new you.

Update your look, your marketing campaign, and start being more consistent on what you are mailing out. I am sure your audience is getting tired of the same old look and routine. Have a blast with it and create something fun!

I love design and being creative! That's why I feel incredibly fortunate to have pursued these passions during my time at the University of North Texas.

My studies there led me to embrace marketing, especially within the realm of real estate, where I've honed essential skills that play a vital role in advancing my career.

Real estate is a boundless realm of possibilities. As an agent, I find myself immersed in multiple overwhelming tasks, from self-promotion to marketing clients' homes and orchestrating their promotion and advertising. The list goes on, as we strive to create our personal brand, forge connections, and expand our reach across various platforms. From online and print advertising to vlogs, podcasts, newsletters, direct mailouts, flyers, brochures, happy hours, movie nights, client appreciation parties, and even sporting events—the avenues are limitless. We'll dive deeper into these aspects in the forthcoming chapters.

In addition to my passion for real estate and marketing, I hold an unabashed admiration for Britney Spears. Some may find it cheesy or argue that she's faced her challenges, but I can't help but be inspired by some of her music, particularly her song "Circus," which, if listened to closely, strikes a chord with real estate. It is this very inspiration that propelled me to write this book.

Real estate agents, just like ringleaders, orchestrate their own circus—putting on a show, taking charge, and cracking the whip to achieve results. We constantly feel the adrenaline moving through our veins, and the spotlight forever shines upon us.

Our clients can vary from wild to tame, and all eyes are on the real estate agent who is initially the ringleader. As we steer toward the desired outcome, it's crucial to always remain at the top of our game, a lesson to bear in mind during every deal we undertake.

Sometimes, we need to muster even greater determination, just like a spinning plate act, keeping several plates aloft simultaneously.

When I think of Britney Spears, I also think of success and wealth. Her staggering net worth of $60 million serves as a motivator for me to strive and achieve financial success in my endeavors. Now, that is a lot of homes to sell. Do what motivates you!

The song "Circus" serves as my anthem, pushing me to gear up, show up, and never give up, no matter how I feel. It kickstarts my day, igniting the motivation to promote myself, expand my business, and make my mark in the real estate domain.

In times of struggle, such as when I was relentlessly studying for my real estate test, I turned to Eminem's powerful hit song, "Lose Yourself." The song's lyrics echoed in my mind:
"If you had one shot or one opportunity to seize everything you ever wanted one moment, would you capture it or just let it slip?"

This mantra drove me forward, reminding me never to surrender and to continue striving for success.

Similar to Britney and Eminem, agents must market themselves effectively. Just as celebrities go all out when releasing an album, we, too, must put in time and effort to market ourselves.

What fuels your passion? What's your source of inspiration? Your spark to perform? What is your song that motivates you?

_____

_____

_____

_____

_____

_____

Marketing Tools

Be innovative and think outside the box when it comes to marketing tools.

Here is a breakdown of some of the marketing tools you will need to incorporate in your business this year.

Photos – Photos play a significant role in shaping our image. If your headshot is outdated, it's time to get a new one. Invest in yourself, as you are the face of your business. Appearance is everything!

Lifestyle shots add depth, capturing moments and scenarios that reflect your personality and brand. Think outside the box and plan for various seasons to showcase different sides of your persona. Bring props and an additional change of clothes so you can use them throughout the year.

A stock of images depicting beautiful homes is a must, too, readily available for your marketing material. Go visit a model home and set up an appointment with a photographer today. Invest in yourself!

Personal brochures—Design and color choices are paramount when creating brochures. Research and explore other agents styles and celebrities' branding to inspire your own unique look. Then collaborate with a talented graphic designer to bring your vision to life.

Once armed with your new photos and striking design, create a personal brochure by selecting some templates from Canva, showcasing testimonials, recent sales, a lifestyle photo, contact information, and your designations. Consider including a smart QR code that records user scans and link that to a personal video. This will allow you to see how many users scan your QR code and other demographic details. You can download QRPics from the Apple store and you can create a custom QR code for yourself. It is amazing!

I have QR codes in my brochures that link to my personal video. That is how I created all the videos throughout this book. Print enough brochures to distribute during open houses, appointments, or community events. You can also create seasonal brochures that detail city events surrounding the various seasonal highlights and holidays.

Similarly, another way to keep your name in front of potential clients is by creating and mailing out "Just Sold" and "Just Listed" cards.

A buyer and listing kit—For those clients whom I know and feel comfortable with, I like to be different. I bought some white boxes and silk ribbon (pink and black) on Amazon that I fill with fun and useful items for my seller, then I drop them off to my listing before the appointment.

Inside the box, I put my brochure on what I do as an agent for my seller, add our company's brand book, personalized tissue paper with my logo on it, a small gift like mints or popcorn, comps, and some closing information. You can even put a QR code sticker on the top of the box and have a personalized video for your buyers or sellers to scan. I like to personalize each one when I have time. You can even create a generic video so you can use it over and over.

Create one today and be different! Make it look like you are giving them a gift.

Personal magazines—You can create your very own personal magazine from Reminder Media by letting them help you create an outstanding publication with your picture and name all over it. I mail out about 25 Smart Healthy magazines at least once a quarter. My clients love these and they have the best recipes in them!

Football schedules—Everyone looks forward to fun mail. For the past 15 years I have been using a company called Magnets USA to create football schedule magnets. I order and mail 100 magnets with The Dallas Cowboys schedule and three college teams on it. On the back is the Monday Night Football schedule. These are great to pass out at open houses too. It is almost a tradition now since I have been mailing these out for so many years.

Sweet treats—I love giving my clients treats. I ordered clear house-shaped acrylic candy boxes and filled them with jellybeans. I also bought some Tic Tac candy and ordered labels from Etsy that said, "You were mint to be a homeowner," with my information on the back of the label. Amazon has everything! Just search real estate agent items and see what you can find that fits your personality.

Do you have client gifts stocked? It's always a good idea to have some items on hand for those rainy, busy days. Stock up on gift cards, create baskets filled with towels, candles, charcuterie boards, décor, etc. World Market and HomeGoods always have the best stuff. Don't forget to explore the exciting range of entertaining gifts and promotional items available at All Things Real Estate on Instagram. They are not your typical real estate store and have everything!

Embrace creativity, build connections, and showcase the unique "You" in every aspect of your real estate journey.

What do you need to create in order to expand your marketing needs?

_____

_____

_____

_____

_____

_____

Five

THE ACROBATIC PERFORMER: THE MANY ACTS OF LOVE

I extend a warm invitation for you to join me on a month-long journey of love on the Trapeze, where we will do tricks and perform solo high-flying acts for our clients. This will definitely be a feel-good show.

L is for the way you look at me,
O is for the only one I see,
V is very, very extraordinary,
E is even more than anyone that you adore can ...

I absolutely adore that enchanting melody made famous by Frank Sinatra! It stirs up a profound feeling of love, and love is indeed a powerful force that can make anything sell, sell, sell!

February – the month in which we celebrate Valentine's Day holds a special place in my heart for marketing. It's an opportune time to shower love on your clients, friends, listings, neighbors and, most importantly, yourself!

Embrace this moment to strengthen relationships and have a blast while doing so. This is where creativity comes into play.

Here are some ideas for you to make the most of this month by planning ahead and strategizing.

Consider the following "Top 10" ideas I've compiled from my own experiences:

1. **Create a marketing piece**—10 Simple Tricks that will make you LOVE your home. Put this in a social media piece.
- Display fresh flowers.
- Make your bed every day.
- Have a clean and organized desk space.
- Limit your laundry.
- Keep floor space clean.
- Declutter.
- Use décor colors that make you happy.
- Keep a happy reading /relaxing space.
- Keep sink areas clean at all times.
- Organize your pantry and refrigerator.

2. **Love on your friends**—Reconnect with friends, family, clients, and neighbors through heartfelt gestures and messages. Call, text, snail mail, video, etc.

For your single friends, send them fun Valentine's cards to brighten their day.

3. **Give LOVE to your listings**—Show your listings some love by ensuring they look their absolute best, and consider adding a touch of romance to your descriptions using ChatGPT. By using this, it will help you come up with the best romance for your listings. It provides you with better words and ideas. Have you used this before? It is amazing!

If your listings need some love, then maybe you need to bring in a stager or some extra items to cheer up the home and make it more inviting. I have a huge bin I carry with me to my vacant listings that contains: throw pillows, candles, fake plants, mirrored trays, towels, cookbooks and knick-knacks. Create yourself a bin. HomeGoods and Target have everything you need.

4. **Host a Valentine's-themed luncheon**—Complete with heart-shaped delicacies and charming decor. Really set the mood. Gather up some fun Valentine's décor and get the party started. Bring in real silverware and real plates and glasses. Make it fancy. You can even drop off special valentine gifts to their neighbors and invite them as well just like you would to an open house.

Here is some help on how to host a Valentine's Luncheon.

Order a salad from your favorite local restaurant, purchase a heart-shaped pizza, grab some chocolate-covered strawberries or heart-shaped cookies for dessert. Maybe even some cranberry mimosas, too!

Create a sign and put it in a picture frame that says, "Fall in LOVE with this beautiful home." Set up is key, so make it look nice. Jazz it up with a nicely decorated red or pink tablecloth and red plates, cups, and napkins. Buy some balloons that are pink, red, and white or have "XOXO" printed on them.

If you really want to go all out for those expensive listings, create a take-home gift for about 15 people. Boxes of chocolates or cookies are a great idea. Little vases with flowers and cute Valentine's plaques with sayings on them are perfect keepsakes.

Another broker luncheon/open house idea is to start using them to hold classes for agents. I hosted a luncheon and taught a Reel class in my last listing. Ask your title company or your lender to help next time you have a listing and see what you can create. This is something I have seen trending and agents really benefit from it. Plus, agents come tour your beautiful listing. It is a win-win! Think outside the box!

5. **Love on your city**—Spread love on social media by expressing your affection for the city you represent and inviting clients and friends to explore it with you.

Tell people where to go and what to do for fun and entertainment in your city. Make a fun "follow me" game on social media. Maybe create a contest or game. I created a Top 10 list of restaurants to take your valentine. It is always a hit, and is very helpful for the guys too so they can make those reservations early.

6. **Surprise your neighbors**—Love on your neighbors with thoughtful pop-by gifts, such as chocolates, hot chocolate in mugs, or delightful treats. Get with a local bakery to help you.

7. **Don't forget your buyers**—Show your appreciation by sending them sweet treats as well.

8. **Host a Galentine's Day party**—(ladies) Celebrate with your 10 closest friends, exchanging notes or Valentine's cards. Create a bag for each person with their name on it. Ask each guest to bring 10, one-dollar items and stuff them in each bag. At the end of the night, you will have 10 gifts to bring home. It is so fun! I did this before and received socks, magnets, candy, earrings, and even a brownie mix.

9. **Love on your family**—Don't forget about your sweet family. Do something special to show your love for them. Have a family brunch, mail them all sweet Valentine's day cards, send a Valentine's day box for adult kids that are in college or married. If you have kids at home, do something fun as a family. Whatever you do just show your love!

10. **Love yourself**—Most importantly, make time for you, and book a self-care day. It could be a spa day, a peaceful walk in nature or any activity that brings you joy.

Let your heart guide you as you embrace creativity, and express love to your clients, friends, listings, neighbors, and yourself.

This month promises to be a delightful journey of spreading love to all. The possibilities are endless during this month.

Get out there and create your own high flying, acrobatic fun. Go through all the hoops for your clients, making sure you love on everyone. XOXO

Six

THE CLOWN CAR: THE ACT OF BALANCING EVERYONE

Clowns are one of the best acts in the circus. I don't know about you, but I love when the clown car comes out. It is always amazing to see how many clowns actually fit in one car. Clowns are always having a good time, making people laugh, and having fun with one another. That is exactly what agents need to be doing. More clowning around with their audience.

Personally, I feel very confident that building and maintaining relationships is crucial for any business, and this is especially true in the real estate industry. These connections often lead to valuable referrals, which we all desire. I cherish the wonderful relationships I've developed over the years, and feel blessed to have many meaningful and genuine friendships.

Working with friends and acquaintances in real estate is something I genuinely enjoy. I believe that working with familiar faces fosters loyalty, and I prefer dealing with my warm market, including my A and B clients, who are the best to collaborate with. That is why it is so important to make those face-to-face meetings.

I've understood the importance of relationships from a young age. Growing up on Keathley Drive in Irving, Texas, I had a close-knit group of friends with whom I shared countless joyful experiences. We did everything from trading stickers and playing hopscotch in the driveway to playing board games like Monopoly, Parcheesi and Chinese checkers. Our time together created lasting memories that I still cherish. These bonds extended to my ballet friends, high school and college buddies, golf companions, neighbors and work colleagues. Despite life taking us in various directions, I've managed to maintain contact with almost all of them.

Staying connected with my vast network does require effort, but it's work I truly appreciate. I keep in touch through texts, regular check-ins, and attending gatherings like happy hours and birthday celebrations. Social media also plays a role in staying connected, as it allows me to share relatable content with my friends and receive their thoughts in return. When someone is going through a tough time, I try to lift their spirits with a thoughtful note, a quick text or a basket of sunshine, following the golden rule of treating others as I would like to be treated.

Create a database—To ensure I stay connected with my network effectively, I have a well-organized database with about 250 people in it, and it has color-coded categories (A, B and C). You want to always start out with your "A" list clients first. These are your best clients, the clients that give you the most business. Every month, I make it a point to reach out to A-list contacts and have a simple conversation without any sales pitch. I record each call and its content, keeping track of my progress to identify any leads.

Then go down the list with your B, C and D clients.

What does your database look like? Do you have a solid one that is updated? What do you use it for? I created mine in Excel and love to print it out and go through it at all times. You need to keep adding to it every month. I had to delete some people over the years, and that is okay. Keep it organized and updated.

Every year around Christmas time is when I really go through it thoroughly because I am about to send everyone a Christmas card. Start adding names and addresses now! Your database could be your next best friend.

Get in your database today and challenge yourself and start making some calls!

Here are some ways to stay connected:

- Make phone calls every day (3).
- Show them they are loved.
- Send gifts or surprise them with something of value.
- Plan a Happy Hour and get everyone together.
- Set up a coffee or lunch date with your A and B clients.
- Have fun with them and send them things on social media.
- Show up for them.
- Text something sweet.
- Pop by and say hi.
- Send them a funny video.

Mailouts / Notes

I am a big fan of mailouts. I didn't always like them but now I try and make it fun. I love sending out Christmas cards. We usually send out over 250 cards every year. We mail them to our friends and our clients. I love to receive them as much as I love sending them. I hope this tradition never fades. I feel like people don't have time for mailing cards anymore and just post them on social media. I love opening each one and reading them and looking at how the family has grown. Please send out your cards; they are so meaningful and thoughtful. Don't let this tradition fade.

Over time, I've attended numerous seminars with some of the best real estate coaches, like Tom Ferry and Brian Buffini, who believe that handwritten notes hold the key to success. Although I write as many notes by hand as possible, the process can sometimes become monotonous.

For years, I wrote handwritten notes, initially focusing on those who were struggling, then reconnecting with old acquaintances, But, eventually, my mind would go blank. I got bored with it.

To infuse some excitement, I decided to make note-writing enjoyable. During Christmas, I initiated a "Secret Santa" exchange with 15 friends and clients, and the experience was delightful. Buoyed by success, I repeated the gesture on Valentine's Day and St. Patrick's Day, dubbing them "Secret Valentine" and "Secret Leprechaun." As the cycle continued, the recipients eventually discovered that I was behind these surprises, but the joy it brought made every effort worthwhile.

Sending out each envelope during these occasions became an eagerly anticipated event for me. I realized that creativity is crucial in all aspects of my life, and infusing it into everything I do adds a sense of fulfillment and enjoyment. I loved hearing from everyone I sent a note to. They all knew it was me. I really enjoyed playing this game with them.

How did I do it?

First, begin by compiling a list of people you want to surprise. In my case, I selected 15 individuals for my Secret Santa. Next, acquire at least 60 colorful envelopes of the same color—I chose pink because that is my favorite color —and pick up some fun Christmas stickers from Hobby Lobby to add a touch of cuteness. Then, proceed to address all 60 envelopes, preparing four envelopes for each of your 15 recipients. (Do not include your return address on the envelopes.) Eventually, every person will receive four surprise notes by mail, resulting in a total of 60 mailouts within a span of two weeks. This initial step takes the most time and effort.

Following that, I create the first note, usually using the excellent design tool, Canva. I highly recommend trying it out; it's user-friendly and enjoyable to learn. Canva is a cloud-based graphic design tool used to create on-brand marketing content, sales presentations, and training videos. Try canva.com and see what you can design.

In the first note, I explain the concept of the surprise and inform recipients that they will be receiving three more letters, each containing surprise gifts. After a three-day interval, I send the second note, then another three days later, the third one, and finally, three days after that, I dispatch the fourth note. The fourth letter is the grand reveal, where I disclose my identity using a QR code I generated with the QRPics app. By the way, this app is also excellent for businesses. This whole process is a lot of fun, and I encourage you to get creative with it. Spread joy and have some lighthearted moments with your friends and clients; they'll love it! Don't forget to include some goodies for the kids; they adore it too. And let's not overlook our furry friends. People love it when you include their pets. And everyone will appreciate the fun in guessing who the sender is.

As for the gift budget, aim for around $150-$200 or less. For instance, I included a free Bundt cake coupon, a $5 Starbucks card, a $2 lotto ticket, plus postage for each note you mail out, estimating an average cost of $10 per person.

Here is a list of items you can send in a regular size envelope in the mail.

- Stickers

- Tea bags

- Bookmarks

- Stamps
- Seeds
- Patches
- Spices
- Recipes
- Fake Tattoos
- Lottery Tickets
- Gift Cards
- Postcards
- Friendship bracelets

Partnerships—Beyond maintaining relationships with friends and clients, I also value my connections with vendors. Building a reliable team of professionals, such as roofers, inspectors, title companies, builders, handymen, lenders, insurance agents, and photographers, enhances my real estate business. Collaborating with them can lead to unique opportunities, like hosting a vendor party for clients or organizing a luncheon for listings. Build your team and let them help you.

Ultimately, every relationship matters in real estate, and I make an effort to connect with everyone I meet, regardless of whether they are potential clients or not. You never know when a casual conversation might lead to a significant business opportunity, as I've experienced firsthand.

Wear your name badge and distribute your business cards to maximize the potential for fruitful collaborations.

In conclusion, clown around and make as many connections as you can. See how many people you can fit in your clown car. Do whatever tricks you have to do to nurture those relationships.

Let your audience experience and feel the love.

This is the foundation of success in the real estate industry. By investing time and effort into these connections, I've seen my business grow, and I cherish the meaningful friendships that have blossomed along the way.

How are you maintaining your relationships? What are you sending to your friends, family, and business connections?

_____

_____

_____

_____

_____

_____

Intermission

Scan to see a personal message from me.

Seven

IT'S SHOWTIME: THE MAGIC ACT OF CELEBRATING YOUR AUDIENCE

*L*et the spectacle commence! Put on your top hat and prepare for exhilarating magic tricks as you embark on a journey to celebrate each and every one of your cherished clients and friends. It's time to shine the spotlight on your clients and put on a show they won't forget. Bring those connections to life and have fun with them. Let the magic begin!

Entertainment is truly my fortè, and I credit my beloved Grandma Johnson for instilling this gift in me. Her impeccable flair for hosting and ensuring everything looked stunning left a lasting impression on me. She was simply perfect in my eyes.

Another influential figure in my life was Peggy Heid, the ultimate party planner. Though she's no longer with us, I owe her a great deal for imparting the art of planning the most unforgettable parties. Her finesse and attention to detail were awe-inspiring. I fondly recall visiting her beautifully decorated Dallas home where she graciously hosted delightful parties, serving the finest food and making everyone feel warmly welcomed.

Peggy was our very own Martha Stewart, and her gatherings were always a joyous affair.

Reflecting on my journey, I believe that if real estate wasn't my calling, I would have likely ventured into the event planning business. Over the past two decades, I have organized numerous events, starting from high school days when I was president of my class to orchestrating golf tournaments and charity events for United Way and Genesis Women's Shelter. I also planned and organized a couple of fashion shows, a clueless scavenger hunt for singles, all-class high school reunions, a Vintage Game Show for real estate agents, and several other events.

Every moment deserves a celebration—Whether it's my friends' or family's birthdays, I try to go all out to make them feel truly special. My belief in creating lasting memories and sharing joy with loved ones is profound. I vividly remember the touching story of a lady friend of mine who had never experienced a birthday party before, reminding myself that everyone deserves to be showered with love and celebration on their special days.

I have embraced the power of sending thoughtful cards as a way to stay connected with your clients. From birthdays to other significant life events like losing a loved one, recovering from illness, welcoming a new baby or getting married, I always make sure to send out heartfelt cards. It's a gesture my clients appreciate, knowing that you remember and care about their important moments.

There are endless occasions for celebrating or encouragement, so stock up on some greeting cards and send them out. The Dollar Tree and Trader Joe's have great cards, and you don't have to pay $5 for them. Cards are getting so expensive these days. I need to go back to making them again.

Client Appreciation Parties

One of the ultimate ways to honor your clients is through a client appreciation party. I try to do one every year.

Here is a list of ideas to help you plan a great client appreciation party: Host a movie day, where you rent out a theater and have your clients come to watch. Or, how about renting out a suite at a local baseball game? Are you a golfer? What about calling a pro-golfer and putting together a lesson for your favorite clients? You can do the same for tennis or even pickleball. Are your client's drinkers? Maybe offer a wine tasting. Do they like to cook? How about a cooking class? There are so many things your clients will love and appreciate. Make sure to create something that you love to do and invite your clients to share your love with you. Not everything has to be a fancy party.

Gobble 'til You Wobble—My passion for entertaining is a little extreme. I love to host! One of my favorite events is my "Gobble 'til You Wobble" party at my home. I tend to go a little overboard on party planning so, if you love to party plan, then you will like this. For my "Gobble 'til You Wobble" party, I invite all my clients and my neighbors, too. I love having everyone over! This event serves as a heartfelt way to express gratitude for the support of my friends and clients over the years, and I usually schedule it right before Thanksgiving. It is a "Thank you for your business and friendship over the years" kind-of-gathering.

Planning such a gathering requires careful attention to detail, and I will generously share with you my tried-and-true steps:

How to throw an event at home:

- Create a guest list of about 40-50 people, including clients and neighbors.

- Design invitations, preferably in snail mail, stating the purpose and theme of the event.

- Organize a "fun wine with a twist" wine tasting, where guests bring their favorite wine for interactive voting.
- Plan a delectable menu, combining homemade dishes and purchased items, ensuring a good mix of finger foods and charcuterie boards.
- Set up a bar area with a variety of drinks, including alcoholic and non-alcoholic options.
- Prepare fall decorations, including crafting numbered wine bags for the wine-tasting game. Pick up a fun prize for the best wine.
- Clean home and start getting ready for the party.

The day before the party, double-check all preparations, set up the tablescape, and arrange the bar area.

On the big day, make sure the house exudes warmth and coziness, with the fireplace ablaze and the patio adorned with freshly washed blankets.

Enjoy the company of your friends and clients, with the help of assistants who will take care of serving and cleaning.

The best and easiest way to prepare food for the party is to have it catered.

For instance, last year we catered in pulled pork with rolls and purchased coleslaw to complement the meal. I also prepared some appetizers while opting to buy a large Thanksgiving charcuterie board. Don't forget to include delicious desserts, but remember to keep it reasonable to avoid having an excessive amount left over.

To minimize last-minute rushing, try making some appetizers the night before the event. This way, you'll have more time to enjoy your guests on the actual day. Once you've decided on your menu, make a shopping list and get all the necessary ingredients and supplies.

A Week Before the Party:

Make a trip to the liquor store to pick up about 15 brown paper wine sacks. After that, head to a craft store to get black paint and white paint. The bags will be used for a fun "wine with a twist" game. Paint black squares on the bags and number them using the white paint. For white wines, attach yellow ribbons, and for red wines, use red ribbons.

On the day of the party, when guests arrive, they can pick a numbered bag and you put the wine inside. Don't let them see which bag their wine is in. Set up a designated table with a Thanksgiving-themed display and provide butcher paper for easy cleanup in case of spills. Have your guests vote on the best wine! Each guest receives a ticket. Have them write the number of their favorite wine on the ticket and put it in a separate wine glass at the end of the table. Then you will find out which number wins.

The Day Before the Party:

Take time to mentally go through your checklist and ensure you have everything you need. If any last-minute items are missing, you still have time to head to the store. Begin setting up the party area by creating a festive tablescape, arranging flowers, and organizing the bar area with all the necessary items.

If you entertain frequently, investing in real plates, silverware, and wine glasses can be advantageous. However, it's a good idea to have paper plates available as well for those who prefer them. Start preparing a few appetizers that you can store in the refrigerator overnight.

The Day of the Party:

Today is the big day! Your house should exude warmth and coziness, with the fireplace on and fresh blankets on the patio. Ensure that the food is already prepared, and you only need to heat it up and set it out for the guests. Play some lively party music and get ready for the festivities. Consider having help to pour wine, clear plates and assist with dishes, allowing you to enjoy the party without too many responsibilities at the end of the night. The extra help is well worth the investment.

Lastly, pull out your magic bag of tricks and treats and start putting something meaningful together for your clients. They will appreciate you, and remember to express your gratitude to your friends for being a part of your life and supporting your business. Capture the special moments of the night with pictures, cherishing the time spent with those who have made your journey in both business and life truly meaningful.

What are you planning on doing for your clients? How are you celebrating and appreciating them?

_____

_____

_____

_____

_____

_____

Eight

BRINGING THE CIRCUS TO YOUR TOWN: THE ACT OF AUDIENCE PARTICIPATION

*B*ring the circus to your community! Gather up your clowns, jugglers, and flying trapeze artists to introduce to your audience in your town and let them see what it all has to offer.

Your community needs you and is calling for your support! As a real estate agent, you hold a position of influence, and people rely on your knowledge of the town. Staying informed about upcoming developments is crucial, as is being aware of local happenings in your neighborhood.

Take this opportunity to expand your network by meeting new people, which can lead to more business opportunities. Even if you're an experienced agent, finding fresh sources of business can be challenging. However, meeting people within your community can open doors.

I think we all got a little too comfortable during COVID and lost touch with some of our friendships, and our community suffered.

Sharing your town with others—Consider sharing exciting news about emerging restaurants, coffee shops or boutiques on social media to network and connect with potential clients. Engaging with local organizations that resonate with your personality is another way to meet like-minded individuals.

Challenge yourself to explore and post about various places in your city, forging new connections along the way. Find a Fantasy football team in your town or create one yourself. How about getting involved more at your church or joining a Bible study? Get involved in a bowling league or at a shooting range. Do you love the theater? See what your town has playing.

There are people everywhere, so get out there and meet them!

Dust off those business cards and distribute them as you venture out with a friend to explore the hidden gems your city has to offer. Or, if you are into those digital business cards, then buy one!

Collaborate with local businesses—Head to your favorite coffee shop, restaurant or boutique, and explore the possibility of having them provide exclusive deals or discounts for your clients.

Building relationships with such establishments can be beneficial for both parties. Create a coffee and real estate networking event and invite some of your top clients and host it at your favorite local coffee shop. I am a big shopper, so I love to do events at boutiques, and maybe the store can offer everyone who comes in and purchases something a special discount in your honor. See how you can help the businesses in your town.

Take action in your community—Engage with your community by getting involved in local charities or volunteer work. Find a cause you are passionate about and invite others to join you in contributing to the cause. For me, I love collecting purses and personal hygiene items for an organization supporting women who are in abusive situations. Last year we were able to stuff over 50 purses. It was amazing to be able to deliver them.

I could barely fit them all in my car. It just takes one person to organize such acts of compassion – let that person be you.

Ebby Halliday, one of the first successful female entrepreneurs in Dallas and founder of Ebby Halliday where I work, has a motto that I love: **"Do something for someone every day."** It's a motto I live by.

Being involved in charitable activities not only helps those in need, but also provides you with a sense of fulfillment and happiness. Pick a charity and get some of your friends together and see what you can do.

Stay informed—As an agent, always stay informed about community events and activities and keep your clients in the loop. Embrace your role as a local expert and share your extensive knowledge with others. Your title company might have valuable information about upcoming events, and sharing these with your clients can foster positive relationships and demonstrate your care for their community experience. For example: Create a list of where to find Bluebonnets, Fourth of July Fireworks, Haunted Houses, Pumpkin Patches, local wineries, etc. Share the list with your clients.

New construction—I have been selling new construction homes since I started in 2000. New homes sales is the way to go, if you sell with the right builder. I really want to encourage you to start selling more new construction. Take some time out and research who is building in your area and go tour those subdivisions. Grab a couple of co-workers and go tour the model homes together and see what the builders have to offer.

Get out there and bring your buyers by to look at the new homes, and strengthen those connections with the sales counselors. They are in their model homes all week waiting to help you.

While you are at the model home, check out the décor and their unique floorplans to see what is trending. There are some great options for building vs buying pre-owned homes.

Find out what incentives they have going on, not only for your buyer but also for you. See if they have any "Partnership Programs" you can take advantage of.

Apartment tours—Apartments can also be an enjoyable and profitable venture. Consider making a list of appealing apartments in your area and take the time to tour them.
Apartment locating can be a lucrative income stream, allowing you to earn a percentage of your tenants' rent.

When I first started real estate, I was in my twenties, and most of my friends were in apartments, so I did bank on bringing my friends to apartments. Don't forget about them!

Focus on doing things that bring you joy and fulfillment. By being an active and engaged member of your community, you will not only enhance your real estate business, but also contribute positively to the lives of others around you. Bring your circus team together and get involved in what makes you happy all while seeing what your city has to offer.

What is your commitment to your community? How can you help your community and get more involved? What can you be sending out to your clients?

_____

_____

_____

_____

_____

_____

Nine

PEANUTS, POPCORN, COTTON CANDY: FUN TREATS AND TRINKETS

*D*uring my childhood, I would always come home from the circus with a little sweet treat or trinket. To me, sweet treats and glow-in-the-dark trinkets were the best part of the circus. You just can't have the full circus experience without trying a couple of these classic timeless delights. With that said, crafting fun pop-by trinkets to give to your clients is a must in real estate.

Pop-bys are one of the aspects of being a real estate agent that I truly enjoy. It allows me to unleash my creativity and engage with both past clients and neighbors. However, the part I'm not so fond of is actually delivering these gifts. If you happen to have an assistant, it's an ideal task for them to handle.

There have been times when some gifts sat on my dining table for months simply because I didn't feel like delivering them or I ran out of time. To avoid overwhelming myself, I find that starting with 10 to 15 pop-bys is a manageable number.

But what exactly are pop-bys, you ask? They are a clever way of connecting with past clients and neighbors by leaving a thoughtful $5-$10 gift on their porches as a way of saying "Hi!"

Throughout the year, I usually plan three or four pop-bys, starting in February with Valentine's Day, and followed by themes for spring, summer and fall. The beauty of pop-bys is that they allow me to get creative according to the seasonal theme and who my clients are.

My favorite and simplest gift involves a roll of wrapping paper tied with a big bow and accompanied by a card expressing thanks for their business or a little something to wrap up their holiday season. I find the best wrapping paper selection at Target. Dropping the gift at their doorstep is a hassle-free approach, and I sometimes add scotch tape and ribbons, which everyone needs during the holidays.

When I plan my pop-bys, I usually start with my neighbors since they're easy to reach. Then, I consider my upcoming travel destinations and think about who I'll be seeing in those areas so I can leave them pop-by gifts.

Pop-bys have proven to be effective marketing tools to generate real estate leads and keep your business in the forefront of your clients' minds. By offering something of value or an item that will sit on their desks, they will often be reminded of you and consider your services when they need a Realtor.

How to create pop-bys—Start by coming up with a catchy slogan. For example, I call February "LOVE month." I find a lifestyle picture of myself in a red outfit and put it on the card/tag, along with a phrase like, "They say diamonds are a girl's best friend, but what about buying a new home?" Then, I create my own tag to attach with a ribbon or glue.

Creating the tags can be done on Canva or Publisher, and you can print them on postcard Avery paper or cardstock and cut them out. After that, I fill the gift bags with fun items, such as a Valentine's coffee cup, heart candy or red and white popcorn.

To assemble the pop-by, I use pretty ribbon to tie the tag to the bag and attach my business card. The personalized pink tissue paper I use complements the Valentine's theme. Once the gift is ready, I follow up with a picture of the bag at their door or even a selfie with me holding the gift on their porch. This gesture helps maintain a personal connection.

Just like the circus when we were little, everyone still appreciates sweet treats and fun trinkets. They never go out of style.

Call me for Pumpkin Spice
and
Real Estate Advice

Ten

THE CONSTANT JUGGLER: THE BALANCING ACTS OF SOCIAL MEDIA

One act I could never literally do was to juggle balls or other objects. No matter how hard I tried I just couldn't do it. I never knew how anyone could juggle so many things all at one time.

Now as an agent, I find it humorous that we are just like that. I mean, how many balls can get thrown at us at the same time? We are constantly juggling.

Social media has become an indispensable tool for promoting businesses. Being absent from these platforms means missing out on potential clients. Social media demands active engagement and a consistent presence. Whether it's through videos, photos or reels, connecting with viewers regularly becomes a habit.

When posting content, it's essential to strike a balance between personal and professional topics. People are more receptive to exciting and beneficial information rather than just constant self-promotion. Make sure what you put on social media is engaging and helpful to your audience.

Pick a platform—Keeping up with social media can feel like a constant juggling act. There are so many platforms to choose from—Facebook, Instagram, LinkedIn, Pinterest, Podcasts, Snapchat, TikTok, Twitter (now called X), and YouTube—that it can be overwhelming. It's essential not to stress about being present on all of them. Instead, focus on a couple of platforms and master them, unless social media is your expertise. For Realtors, you need to concentrate on Instagram and Facebook.

If you are really talented, you may want to create your own YouTube channel where you post "How To" videos pertaining to real estate, or create videos that answer questions for buyers or sellers. YouTube is just fascinating to me and I hope one day to have my channel up and running successfully. Maybe even a podcast! #goals

Finding content—For real estate agents, social media can be particularly challenging, given busy schedules with buying and selling homes. It is hard to carve out time for this. If you can't do it naturally, then hire someone to help you do your social media for you.

Alternatively, invest time in learning how to enhance your social media posting skills. One great resource for inspiration is Pinterest, where you can find a plethora of fun and engaging content ideas. The platform offers various lists and calendars that you can follow to maintain a consistent posting schedule.

Suggestions for what to post on social media:

- Promote upcoming events in your town

- Client testimonials

- Go LIVE one day.

- Mini lesson on something real estate related

- Run a giveaway.

- Tuesday Tip or Friday Facts

- Thankful Thursday's

- Share a funny real estate story.
- Give a shoutout to a local business.
- Tips on how to make your house cozier
- Share an inspiring story.
- Educate your viewers about your industry.
- Share a book you're reading.
- Holiday fun
- Post your favorite recipe.
- Ask what their favorite restaurant is in your town.
- Home maintenance tips
- Home projects that are trending.

There is so much out there for you to post for your viewers. Give Pinterest a try and see what you can come up with.

Creating boards on Pinterest is a personal favorite of mine. Whenever I come across something that I want to share with others, I save it to a relevant board, such as my real estate board or other categories like healthy foods, shopping, parties, beach, Bible quotes, detox, dream home, holidays, and more.

By exploring what Pinterest has to offer, you can find countless ideas that will spark your creativity and help you create captivating content for your social media platforms.

Video content—is crucial for real estate agents. Practice and improve your video skills, showcasing properties, answering common questions for buyers and sellers or giving virtual tours. I know not everyone likes to do videos. I am not even a big fan, but you have to do it. Viewers like videos.

Try and get comfortable on the camera and start with a few videos of you answering some questions regarding real estate. Questions like, "What is the option period?" How much does a buyer need to put down on a house? What are the interest rates now? What is the market doing in your area? Educate your viewers on the knowledge you have and create some content!

Personal videos—It is important to create a personal video to showcase what you do in the city you sell in. Hire a videographer, write out a script, and let your viewers see you in action. Ask a couple of your clients or vendors to be in the video with you to provide a testimonial about you and your services.

Finding the right equipment—Having good equipment, such as a quality phone, ring light, and microphone, can significantly enhance the quality of your videos. You can buy all these products on Amazon.

You don't have to get the most expensive items – just get the basics and start doing some videos. Post them on the platforms you are comfortable with first.

Hashtags—Hashtags are an essential tool for categorizing and tracking content on social media platforms. They help individuals post to reach a broader audience interested in specific topics. Using relevant hashtags, such as #newlisting #realtor #realestate #buyersagent #listingagent, can boost the visibility of your posts. Put in as many hashtags as you want describing the content you are posting.

Engaging with your friends—Social media is an excellent medium for connecting with people, allowing agents to interact with clients, friends and colleagues. Responding to messages and engaging with comments can foster stronger relationships and build trust with your audience.

However, it's essential to be mindful of the time spent on social media to avoid distractions.

Marketing your properties—Social media is a great means for you to show off your listings, introduce yourself as a real estate professional and educate your viewers on the housing market.

I love to create Reels on every one of my listings! I show off pictures of the home in my videos to all my media platforms as an effective means of advertising. This is why it is important to follow other Realtors on social media so you can interact with them and hopefully make a sale. Go through and find agents and add them as your friend. Don't forget about your builders, too. Head out to explore and create some fun videos by touring subdivisions and new home sites.

It is a great marketing tool for all.

Think about others and be kind—Consider using social media to showcase more than just your own achievements. Highlight your clients' successes, feature local businesses, or share useful information about the market and the community you serve. Help your friends out in their business. Don't forget about your co-workers by sharing their new listings. It can be a win-win!

It doesn't always have to be about you. Everyone already knows who you are and that you are a real estate agent.

Use social media to help others. Don't make it all about yourself.

Overall, social media is a powerful tool that is here to stay. Embrace it, have fun with it, and continue finding creative ways to connect with your audience and promote your real estate business.

Don't let it scare you or overwhelm you. Just be yourself and have some fun.

Juggle what you can. Sometimes you just have to take risks! Be yourself and have some fun with social media.

"THE BIGGEST RISK IS NOT TAKING ANY RISK. IN A WORLD THAT'S CHANGING QUICKLY, THE ONLY STRATEGY THAT'S GUARANTEED TO FAIL IS NOT TAKING RISKS."

-Mark Zuckerberg

21 Day Challenge

- [ ] Write 5 note cards a week
- [ ] Do two open houses
- [ ] Create a fun social media piece
- [ ] Create a video or reel for social media
- [ ] Prepare 5 Buyer packets
- [ ] Prepare 5 Listing packets
- [ ] Tour a new subdivision and post about out
- [ ] Go tour one of the best apartment complexes in your city
- [ ] Go to a network event
- [ ] Start reading a real estate book
- [ ] Go buy a new work outfit
- [ ] Clean your lockboxes
- [ ] Ask 5 people for a Referral
- [ ] Clean out your car
- [ ] Get your desk organized
- [ ] Volunteer at a local charity and meet new people
- [ ] Prospect
- [ ] Go through all your leads and make some phone calls
- [ ] Get a Listing
- [ ] Get a new Buyer
- [ ] Organize your folders on your computer

Eleven

WALKING THE TIGHTROPE: THE ULTIMATE CHALLENGES OF REAL ESTATE

Real estate can be just like the dangerous acts of fire breathing, wall of death or sword swallowing. I mean, it is not always that crazy, but still we have to walk those tightropes carefully and learn how to survive in the market.

My biggest challenge in real estate was in 2008, when the housing market bubble burst with subprime mortgages, a huge consumer debt load and crashing home values converged. It was terrible for everyone in the industry. Homeowners began defaulting on their home loans, causing us to be in a recession.

I remember having three closings that year and having my brother and his girlfriend move into my house to help me with bills.

Trying to navigate my next move to figure out how to receive income flowing again was causing major stress.

Luckily, for me, a new sports bar was opening up close to my Ebby office and I got a job there. And just like that, I was back to cocktailing and waiting tables again.

I thought at 35 years old I was done with serving drinks but, thankfully, it didn't last too long.

Dallas Morning News even wrote an article about real estate agents having to get out of the industry and find other means of income. Guess who was on the cover of the paper serving drinks? I was mortified! "Why am I going backwards?" I thought to myself. I did what I had to do to survive and I am so happy that I had income coming in again.

I actually enjoyed those nine months serving drinks. I met a lot of The Dallas Stars players and even made some friends that I eventually sold homes to down the road.

Being an agent definitely presents its fair share of challenges, and one of the toughest aspects is maintaining discipline amidst numerous distractions throughout the day.

With various tasks and responsibilities pulling you in different directions, staying focused can be quite daunting. Unlike a typical 9-to-5 desk job, real estate agents work tirelessly, often throughout the week and on weekends, showing homes, attending listing appointments, meetings and educational classes. We also handle inspections, among other tasks.

The need for effective prioritization and planning becomes paramount in such a dynamic environment, where there's always something demanding your attention, from luncheons with builders to expiring option periods or potential buyer offers. It is never-ending.

Setting boundaries—We all need to set boundaries and seek help when necessary. Setting boundaries is crucial in this business.

Here are a couple things I do that give me peace.

1. I don't look at my phone at dinner. That is family time.

2. When I am on vacation, I usually ask a co-worker to help me if I am busy.

3. I usually turn off my phone around 9 p.m. until 8:30 the next morning.

4. I try to check my emails in the morning, after lunch, and after 5 p.m., unless I am at my desk or waiting for something important. It seems I am always waiting on someone.

5. If I tend to get overwhelmed, I ask myself, "What is the most important task for the day?" Then I tackle it. You can't be everywhere at all times. Prioritize your day!

6. Don't get overwhelmed! Do what you can do and try not to overcommit.

7. Say no to things you don't really need to do.

8. Give yourself breaks.

9. Spend time with your friends and family.

10. Take care of yourself and have your massage therapist on speed dial.

What boundaries do you need to set?

_____

_____

_____

_____

_____

_____

Multiple party transactions—Another act that is challenging is managing a real estate transaction that involves a multitude of players; From buyers and sellers to real estate agents, title companies, lenders, brokers, developers, insurance agents, assistants, transaction coordinators and property managers, the list seems never-ending.

Each transaction can sometimes involve up to eight different individuals, and when you have four transactions occurring simultaneously, it becomes quite a challenge. Try to keep it all straight by writing down everyone involved in your client's folder.

Seek help—During 2021, I faced the demanding task of handling around 12 transactions, all in various stages, all at the same time without any assistance. This workload led me to seek the help of a transaction coordinator to ensure everything ran smoothly. Transaction coordinators prove to be extremely valuable in such situations. Try and find yourself a good one.

Taking diligent notes on each transaction is crucial to keep track of the people involved. Avoiding confusion and preventing any mishaps is of utmost importance in this line of work, as multiple parties are invariably involved in every transaction. Make sure you keep track of everyone.

When the pace is slow—However, there are periods when the pace slows down, and despite the relief of catching up on paperwork and marketing during such weeks, it can also feel disheartening.

Going from juggling multiple clients to seemingly having nothing can lead to self-doubt and a sense of inadequacy. This can be very challenging for not only seasoned agents but new agents too.

During these moments, it's crucial to remind oneself to take a breath, pause and accept that it's okay to have slower times in the real estate business. It is okay to just be still. You don't have to always be crazy busy. Don't burn yourself out and always be protective of your energy. Keep working hard and stay focused. Remind yourself that you are doing exactly what you should be doing. Stay positive!

Take a break and treat yourself to a Hallmark movie to relax and chill out! If business is slow, then planning a vacation can be rewarding. They always say if you are slow, plan a trip because that is when you get busy. But remember, get someone to help you while you are away so you can unplug and enjoy your friends and family.

Sometimes slow is good. It gives you the opportunity to get caught up on all the things you have been procrastinating over the last months.

Lastly, NEVER compare yourself to anyone; everyone is in different seasons in life. This is very common for agents to do but focus on what you need to be doing, not anyone else.
Success is what you make of it, it's not all about what is in your bank account and who is number one. Each agent's journey is unique, and it's essential to be kind to yourself, recognizing your accomplishments and progress.

Don't undervalue yourself and make sure to reward and celebrate your success. Remember success cannot come without failure.

The 21-Day Challenge—To help reignite the drive, a practical approach is the "21-Day Challenge."

Create a list of 21 tasks that need to be accomplished within the next three weeks or 21 days, customizing it to your specific needs and goals.

This challenge not only fosters productivity but also helps in forming positive habits over time.

Grab a pen and paper and start brainstorming your personalized challenge, outlining the necessary actions and steps to move your real estate endeavors forward. Remember, everyone experiences slower periods, and avoiding burnout is crucial for long-term success in the real estate industry.

Here is your 21-Day Challenge

- Write 5 note cards a week and mail them.
- Conduct two open houses.
- Create a fun social media piece.
- Create a video or REEL for social media.
- Prepare 5 buyer packets.
- Prepare 5 listing packets.
- Tour a new subdivision and post about it.
- Go tour one of the best apartment complexes in your city.
- Go to a networking or chamber event.
- Start reading a real estate book.
- Buy a new work outfit.
- Clean your lockboxes.
- Ask 5 people for a referral.
- Clean out your car.
- Get your desk organized.
- Volunteer at a charity and meet new people.
- Prospect for new clients.
- Go through your database and make three phone calls a day.
- Get a listing.
- Get a new buyer.
- Organize your folders on your computer.

Take time out and get it done! You will sleep better.

I challenge you to create your own list and see what you can come up with.

Type up your list and print it out so it is in front of you at all times. Maybe even give it to another co-worker as an accountability partner and challenge them and do it together. I promise you will feel better when you accomplish everything you cross off your list.

The Stick Game—I also play another game too. If I don't make it fun, then I won't do it. I call it my stick game. Some people make fun of me and some call me brilliant. I guess it just all depends on your personality. It is even great for kids.

Here's what I do for the stick game:

I go to a craft store and buy a bag of tongue depressors or popsicle sticks and I write down 21 things I need to be doing. Then, each day I pull one stick out and I have 24 hours to complete that task. I have everything from household chores to exercises to work stuff. If I do all my sticks, my house is cleaned and my work is completed. PLUS: I did more workouts than normal, so I am happy about that! You can either roll your eyes or go buy your sticks and get things done. It's totally up to you!

Don't Be Among the 87% of Real Estate Agents Who Fail!

I always tell new agents that they need to run their business like they own a boutique. If you owned your own boutique, would you only work a couple of hours there? No, you would work there all day!

Being a good agent takes a lot of courage, discipline, focus and a healthy mindset. Yes, you will face many challenges in this industry, but that will make you stronger.

Remember, when you are ready to walk the tightrope make sure to plan out your days, make appointments and get your act together. Don't get stuck creating bad habits.

You can do it! Challenge yourself and create change. You have the power to create the life you want!

Twelve

THE GRAND FINALE:
THE FINAL FAREWELL

As this circus act is is ending on this end, the show must still go on in your business. It is time for a final review, the grand finale, before you leave the Big Top.

Are you ready to divide and conquer and get back to the basics?

In these closing moments, I'd like to share with you some final thoughts that could greatly benefit your business.

I understand you might not be able to do everything in this book. In fact, it was not my intention that you should. I don't want to add more stress to your life; I simply want to give you some ideas that might be helpful. If you can incorporate even a few of my ideas into your busy life, that is better than doing nothing at all.

My primary aim is to inspire you to take action, get more creative, and get out there and make things happen. You are the only one who can do it! I am proud of you for taking this step to help yourself!

Life is all about Balance

"REMEMBER, YOU DON'T ALWAYS NEED TO BE GETTING STUFF DONE. SOMETIMES IT'S PERFECTLY OKAY, AND ABSOLUTELY NECESSARY, TO SHUT DOWN, KICK BACK, AND DO NOTHING."

~ Lori Deschene

Make sure you are keeping your spirits up when entering a burnt-out state. If you find yourself in that situation, then it is time to make some changes in your business because you need some help.

Here are some ways to help keep you from spinning out of control:

- Work better on your time management.

- Hire a transaction coordinator/assistant.

- Slow down.

- Take time for yourself.

- Schedule time for what is needed.

- Exercise/pray/meditate.

- Stay healthy.

- Get organized.

- Work *Life *Balance

- Choose calm over chaos.

- Stay positive.

- Create a notebook to write everything down in one place.

- Reach out if you need help.

- Watch your words when frustrated.

Staying Professional

I have worked with a lot of agents over the years and I have witnessed a lot of bad behavior. Over the past couple years, it seems to be getting worse. Stay educated, stay on top of the market, and know what you are doing. If you don't know what you're doing, then ask for help and seek a mentor.

Here are some things to do and not to do.

Etiquette for Real Estate Agents

- Don't overcommit. It is okay to say "NO."

- Don't let other agents bully you.

- Don't let your clients run your life.

- Don't trash talk other agents.

- Protect your energy.

- If you do commit to something, keep that commitment.

- Don't try to do more than you can – it makes you look bad when you start forgetting and overcommitting. It makes you look unorganized.

- Use a calendar and write everything down.

- Always seem put together and ahead of the game.

- Never say, "I am so busy."

- Be prepared.

- Remember etiquette when showing a listing. Be on time, lock all doors, and always provide feedback. Leave the house the way you found it.

- Return calls and text back.

- Don't be immature—no ghosting.

- Always be sure to respond back to everyone.

- Dress professionally when showing homes and attending closings.
- Remember to check your voicemails.
- Make arrangements before going out of town.
- Stay educated.
- Stay organized.
- Always provide your clients with beneficial information.
- Use your database.
- Always be meeting new people in your community and socializing.
- Always know the market you sell in.
- Always be on time to appointments even if your clients are always late.

Real estate can be a very rewarding career. I have really enjoyed many years of it, and I love the flexibility it offers. I hope you enjoyed all my ideas I shared with you in this book.

My goal was to provide and train you to get out there and do something creative. Whether you are a seasoned agent or new agent, it can be tough going back to the basics.

Be prepared for the crazy time during the slow times, stay organized, create good routines and good habits, get out in your community and go explore what your city has to offer, keep those connections strong with everyone, throw an event for your clients and most importantly celebrate everyone.

It is time for you to shine, so get out there and master your own circus. Be the best ringleader you can be. The spotlight is on you.

What are some takeaways from this book? What do you need to do? If you can pick 5 ideas from this book that you could put into practice for yourself, what would they be?

_____

_____

_____

_____

_____

_____

Scan to see a personal message from me.

I would love to hear what you liked most
about this book. Email and let me know how you liked it.
Also, email me if you have any questions that I can help with.
Also visit my website for more info.
Good luck to you!

Facebook-
https://www.facebook.com/lisa.johnson.104

Instagram-
https://www.instagram.com/ljohnson3333/

Website- Lisajohnsonrealtor.com

Email- Prosperhomegirl@gmail.com

Lisa Johnson Juden

About the Author

Meet Lisa Johnson Juden, a Top Producer with an impressive 23-year career dedicated to serving the DFW real estate, assisting both buyers and sellers. Her outstanding success in the industry has led her to venture into writing a book tailored for real estate agents. Driven by her genuine passion for her colleagues' growth and prosperity, Lisa offers valuable advice, helpful tips, and creative tricks, aiming to inspire agents to embrace the fundamentals of real estate in an enjoyable and innovative manner.

Lisa's achievements in real estate have garnered her recognition and accolades. She has been featured several times in prominent publications like *D Magazine* honoring her as best real estate agent and even appeared on HGTV's House Hunters, she also has her own show on Reveel network called Negotiators Luxe. Her expertise has also led her to serve on various advisory boards throughout her successful career.

Among her many accolades, Lisa remains in the top 20 in her Frisco office, on her company's honor roll and was presented with a VIP customer service award, highlighting her commitment to providing exceptional service for her clients.

Residing in Prosper, TX, Lisa is married to Edward Juden and has three beautiful stepdaughters Lauren, Brooke and Taylor.

Notes